Aquarium on WHEELS

Rob Waring, *Series Editor*

NATIONAL GEOGRAPHIC
LEARNING

Australia · Brazil · Mexico · Singapore · United Kingdom · United States

Words to Know

This story is set in the United States. It takes place in the state of Maryland, in the city of Baltimore.

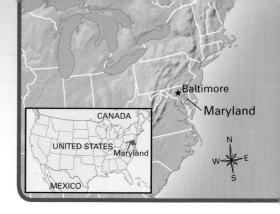

 An Aquarium. Read the paragraph. Then complete the sentences with the correct form of the <u>underlined</u> words or phrases.

People usually visit the National <u>Aquarium</u> in Baltimore, Maryland, to see fish and other <u>marine</u> life. However, this institution also has a special program which takes science out of the <u>laboratory</u> and brings it to the public. School <u>program coordinators</u> work with local teenagers to transport aquarium exhibits to area locations. They travel to schools and libraries to teach children about <u>marine biology</u> and conservation plans.

1. _____ refers to something from or related to the sea.

2. _____ are places where one can learn about life in water.

3. _____ is the study of living things in the sea.

4. _____ plan and organize special events and activities.

5. _____ are places where scientists research and study.

Aquarium

Aquarium on Wheels

B **Tropical Rain Forests.** Read the paragraph. Then match word with the correct definition.

   Tropical rain forests receive at least 250 centimeters* of rain a year and are found in many places in the world. Animals, such as poison dart frogs, monkeys, and snakes, depend on the rain forests for survival. However, these days, many animal and plant species are endangered due to the loss of rain forests. As a result, there's been an enormous movement around the world to help the rain forests through conservation programs.

*See page 24 for a metric conversion chart

1. tropical rain forest _____	**a.** a thick forested area with high temperatures and heavy rains
2. poison dart frog _____	**b.** huge; very big
3. species _____	**c.** a small, brilliantly colored animal with a large mouth and long, powerful legs
4. enormous _____	**d.** a specific group of living things that has similar characteristics

monkey

A Tropical Rain Forest

poison dart frog

In a classroom at the National Aquarium in the city of Baltimore, ten high school students are preparing for a lesson. The group is going through exhibit articles as part of their research. As the group's leader starts examining the items, she offers suggestions about how the items might be used in a classroom. The students seem to enjoy the preparation and review time before their lesson starts, but this is not preparation for just any class. These students are preparing to be teachers. They're collecting information about tropical rain forests so that they can then teach younger children about conservation.

Once they've finished their lesson plans, the teens begin gathering various samples of wildlife in the Aquarium's laboratory. "Where's the poison dart frog container?" says their leader as they begin putting their living samples into transportable cases. The cases are part of a **show-and-tell**[1] presentation for children at public libraries throughout the Baltimore area. The students are also creating **costumes**[2] for a play that they've written which they are planning to perform later that day. Due to the age of the participants, this preparation and planning appears to be schoolwork, but it isn't. In fact, these students are actually working at jobs that have been especially designed for students. They are employees of a very special program called 'Aquarium on Wheels.'

---

[1]**show-and-tell:** a classroom activity in which each person gives information about an object they have brought with them
[2]**costumes:** special clothing worn by an actor or for entertainment

 CD 3, Track 03

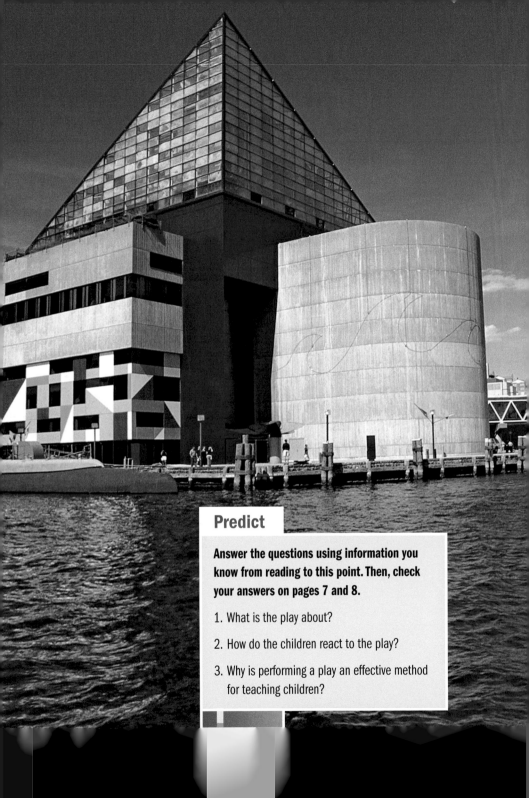

Predict

Answer the questions using information you know from reading to this point. Then, check your answers on pages 7 and 8.

1. What is the play about?

2. How do the children react to the play?

3. Why is performing a play an effective method for teaching children?

As the group moves out to take the aquarium to a new set of viewers, one student employee explains the concept behind the program. "There are a lot of kids who do not have the opportunity to come to the aquarium," she explains "[They don't get] to see live animals or anything like that, so we bring the aquarium to them." This group of young educators brings the aquarium to schools and libraries around the city by van. As they do so, they pack and unpack the van with marine plants and animals each time they stop, which is why the program has earned the name 'Aquarium on Wheels.'

The overall objectives of Aquarium on Wheels are to **entertain**[3] and educate. Each year, though, Aquarium on Wheels has an additional specific goal. This year's goal is to explain the importance of the world's rain forests to young people. Through their plans, the student teachers want to help their young audience to better understand conservation. As part of the educational program, the members have written an interactive play for children about why it is essential for rain forests to survive. The students are even using their time and creativity to perform the play. They're playing the roles of various rain forest animals, such as monkeys and birds, to help young children to better understand their message.

---

[3]**entertain:** amuse; maintain interest through fun activities

The play begins with one of the actors wearing a monkey costume and speaking to a young woman in front of a rain forest background. The monkey is a species that is directly threatened by the destruction of the rain forest because it relies on the leaves that the rain forest provides for food. When the woman informs the monkey actor that people are going to cut down one of the nearby trees, the monkey becomes very upset. As part of the play, the young actor replies, "They're going to cut down this tree? How am I going to find my leaves to eat?" He then continues while the children watch him closely, "That means I'm going to have to fight other monkeys! I can't fight other monkeys; I'm going to **mess up**[4] my hair!" As he says this, the actor reaches up and combs through the hair on his monkey costume and the children laugh and smile.

Plays are an entertaining and interesting method of involving children in local schools and libraries in the educational process. They're also an excellent way to make the destruction of the rain forest more realistic for these children. By helping these young people to learn how to care, it may eventually help these animals and plants that may soon be endangered.

_____

[4]**mess up:** make dirty or untidy

For the young student employees who wrote, directed, and starred in the play, the program is about more than just amusing the children. Later, the actor who plays the role of the monkey explains the serious environmental message that the play holds. "We're trying to get through to the kids that saving one tree can be important to all the animals in the rain forest," he states.

For aquarium **administrators**,[5] on the other hand, the program is about more than just teaching biology, or even teaching about the environment; it's about offering student employees lessons for life. Martha Schaum is the program coordinator at the aquarium. "Most kids like to play in the water—let's be realistic," she explains. "So marine biology is a really great **vehicle**[6] to use [in order] to teach the other skills that they need to know."

---

[5]**administrator:** a person who supervises or manages
[6]**vehicle (noun):** a means or method for doing something

One set of skills that the high school students need are the communication skills that are necessary to get and keep a job. Some of the young people working on the program are now—or may someday be—trying to get accepted into college. All of them need to know how to apply and conduct themselves in an interview for work or school. In other words, the students need the skills necessary to succeed in their lives.

Schaum explains that it's all a matter of offering the students the right encouragement, and a lot of support. She says, "I think for many of them—probably for most of them—they are probably the first in their family to go to college. So what we're doing is coming behind them and saying, 'You can do it!'"

For the student workers, it seems that one of the main lessons that they learn through the program is a sense of duty. They gain a feeling that they are responsible for teaching the younger kids about important issues. "I wouldn't be the person I am today if it wasn't for them," explains one of the student employees. "Basically, they taught me responsibility. That's a big thing I've learned here."

As the play finishes and the student instructors begin the show-and-tell part of their lesson, it becomes obvious how much work went into the project. The students are very knowledgeable about both the rain forest and the various animals which they have brought with them. Schaum explains that the students assumed the entire responsibility for the rain forest project from the start. The students themselves had to plan and organize it, she reports, and they had to learn how to become teachers. "They knew we were going to discuss the rain forest," she explains. "That's a big **topic**[7]. They had to decide how they wanted to present it, the concept that they wanted to use. They had to write the **script**[8]. They had to decide the sorts of things they wanted in the lab[oratory]." Through this work, the student teachers learned an enormous amount about organization and planning, and they also learned a bit about themselves as well.

---

[7]**topic:** a subject of attention, writing, or conversation; a field
[8]**script:** a text for a play

These young teachers are positively influencing the children they teach and having a positive effect on the younger generation. In addition, they are helping their local community through their educational program as well. As student teachers begin to realize these two facts, it often helps them to grow as people and become more adult. More importantly, it helps them to build their **self-esteem**.[9]

The students' growing confidence and self-esteem becomes apparent in a number of ways. One of the most important is in how the student teachers feel about themselves and their teaching experience. "It means a lot to me," says one of the participants. "I have been here for three years and I really feel like I have helped a lot of people understand conservation." However, for many of these teenagers, the real value of Aquarium on Wheels is more personal; it's about their own dreams for their lives. For many, their experience with the aquarium helps them to decide what they want to study in college and where they want to go in their future careers.

---

[9]**self-esteem:** a feeling of liking oneself; a sense of self-worth

It's no surprise that many of the high school students want to work in the fields they've learned so much about —marine biology or conservation. One group member says, "At first it just seemed like a really cool job to work at the aquarium. Now that I've been working here, I've finally found out what I want to be. I've found out that I want to be a marine biologist." Another member adds, "I want to be an environmental lawyer, so it helps me out a lot." And yet another says, "The program really means a lot to me because I want to **major in**[10] marine biology. And here at the aquarium I can get the experience that most other students wouldn't be able to receive." The program is proving to be advantageous for these students in helping them to prepare for their future professional lives.

As the team of young teachers wraps up their program for the day, their young audience applauds happily. For the student teachers, the program is a satisfying way for them to earn money and prepare for their futures. For Martha Schaum, the program allows her to achieve personal and professional satisfaction from watching these teenagers grow as people. She is thrilled to know that she has helped them to become more responsible adults. "This program has meant more to me than anything else," she shares, "because I have watched these kids grow and develop." The Aquarium on Wheels program is having a powerful impact on more than just the rain forests, it's having a positive effect on everyone involved with this very special program.

---

[10]**major in:** focus one's studies on

Summarize

Imagine you are a newspaper or radio reporter. Write or tell a story about Aquarium on Wheels. Include the following information:

1. What are the benefits of the program for the children being taught?

2. What are the benefits of the program for the student teachers?

3. What are the benefits of the program for the school administrators?

After You Read

1. Which is NOT a part of the students' preparation for show-and-tell?
   A. making costumes
   B. gathering information
   C. starting a school
   D. performing a play

2. In paragraph 1 on page 7, 'them' refers to:
   A. animals at the aquarium
   B. children who can't go to the aquarium
   C. student employees
   D. students at the aquarium

3. According to the writer, what are the two goals of Aquarium on Wheels?
   A. perform and educate
   B. help and understand
   C. amuse and entertain
   D. educate and entertain

4. Saving _____ one tree is good for all the animals in the rain forest.
   A. another
   B. every
   C. each
   D. just

5. What does Martha Schaum think the program is about?
   A. saving the monkeys in the rain forest
   B. helping children understand biology
   C. teaching responsibility to teenagers
   D. using biology as a vehicle for teaching conservation

6. According to Schaum, why is marine biology a good way to teach skills?
   A. College is a vehicle for learning.
   B. Students can enjoy and learn at the same time.
   C. Communication is important for work.
   D. Students like to swim.

7. In paragraph 2 on page 12, 'we're' refers to:
   A. aquarium administrators
   B. the rain forest project team members
   C. the young teachers
   D. adults in general

8. Which is a suitable heading for page 12?
   A. The Rain Forest Play
   B. Learning New Jobs
   C. Students Can Do It
   D. No Responsibility

9. In paragraph 2 on page 16, the word 'experience' is closest in meaning to:
   A. job and money
   B. skills and knowledge
   C. help and knowledge
   D. feeling and events

10. What personal benefit has the program given many of the student employees?
   A. a great first job
   B. some money
   C. knowledge about conservation
   D. a direction for their future plans

11. The writer would probably describe Martha Schaum as:
   A. discreet
   B. thrilling
   C. rewarding
   D. satisfied

12. What is the main purpose of this story?
   A. to show that kids like aquariums
   B. to teach about marine biology
   C. to explain a special program
   D. to introduce career options

FAQ: *Frequently Asked Questions* about **Ethiopia Reads**

WHAT IS ETHIOPIA READS?

Ethiopia Reads is an organization which aims to help young Ethiopians learn to read, and to create a culture of reading in Ethiopia. It seeks to achieve these goals by providing quality reading materials in locations that are readily accessible to all children, while providing supportive adult guidance.

HOW DID ETHIOPIA READS BEGIN?

While working at the San Francisco Public Library, Yohannes Gebregeorgis, a native of Ethiopia, was unable to find any books in the 83-plus Ethiopian languages. He realized that Ethiopian children urgently needed books in order to learn to read, so he asked author Jane Kurtz for help. Kurtz, who has lived in Ethiopia and authored several books for children, worked with local organizations in Grand Forks, North Dakota, to raise money for the project. The program was started with these contributions, and others from the San Francisco Public Library.

WHERE DO THE BOOKS COME FROM?

Materials in local Ethiopian languages, such as textbooks, reference books, and story books, are purchased from local publishers or published by Ethiopia Reads. Since English is the language used in most high schools and for university placement exams, the libraries also offer English language books. Some of these books are purchased, but many are donated by people in English-speaking countries and shipped directly to Ethiopia Reads.

Challenges Faced by Ethiopia Reads

- 58% of Ethiopians age 15 and above cannot read.

- Classes in government schools typically have approximately 180 students.

- At present, 99% of schools in Ethiopia have no libraries.

The Donkey Library

Ethiopia Reads has found a unique way to meet the needs of residents living in the farming region around Awassa. In 2006, they began using a donkey cart to transport books to children who had no libraries in their neighborhood. 'Queen Helina,' as the donkey is called, brings books to thousands of children who would not usually have access to them.

The Ethiopia Reads' Queen Helina and Her Transportable Library

HOW SUCCESSFUL ARE THE LIBRARIES?

In 2003, Ethiopia Reads opened the country's first free library for children in downtown Addis Ababa. The Shola Children's Library now contains 50,000 books and provides a safe, well-organized, environment in which children can read, study, and learn. More than 200,000 children have visited the library, which is open six days a week, since 2003. In addition, the organization has opened ten branch libraries in other districts of the city and has plans to open 100 libraries, including sites in all eight major cities, by the year 2010.

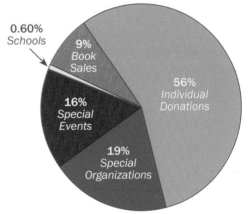

0.60% Schools
9% Book Sales
56% Individual Donations
16% Special Events
19% Special Organizations

Ethiopia Reads Funding Sources

CD 3, Track 04

Word Count: 381
Time: _____

Vocabulary List

administrator (11, 19)
aquarium (2, 4, 7, 11, 16, 18, 19)
costume (4, 8)
enormous (3, 15)
entertain (7, 8)
laboratory (2, 4, 15)
major in (18)
marine (2, 7)
marine biology (2, 11, 18)
mess up (8)
poison dart frog (3, 4)
program coordinator (2, 11)
script (15)
self-esteem (16)
show-and-tell (4, 15)
species (3, 8)
topic (15)
tropical rain forest (3, 4)
vehicle *(noun)* (7, 11)

Metric Conversion Chart

Area
1 hectare = 2.471 acres

Length
1 centimeter = .394 inches
1 meter = 1.094 yards
1 kilometer = .621 miles

Temperature
0° Celsius = 32° Fahrenheit

Volume
1 liter = 1.057 quarts

Weight
1 gram = .035 ounces
1 kilogram = 2.2 pounds